WELCOME

When it comes to capturing the zeitgeist, few bands can claim to have done so as effectively as Oasis. Through a blend of raw, anthemic lyrics and instantly memorable melodies, five Mancunian lads embodied the hopes and fears of millions of like-minded youngsters in the mid-90s, propelling them to global fame at a time of musical and political upheaval. Triumphing against impossible odds, in a few short years Oasis went from playing in half-empty bars to commanding a crowd of over 100,000 at Knebworth and racking up record-breaking album sales. With nothing but their own talent and towering ambition, they battled their way to unfathomable heights, breaking new ground and stamping an indelible imprint on rock 'n' roll. Their songs remain seared into the memories of a legion of fans who see themselves reflected in the precocious rockers to this day, a testament to the phenomenon that is Oasis, a band unlike any other, one shaped by controversy, rivalry, and above all an endless drive to create music that stirs the soul. This is their story.

Image: Kevin Cummins / Getty

The air inside the three-storey Boardwalk nightclub was thick with smoke and the smell of booze as a lean, tousle-haired lad strutted out onto the stage and adjusted the mic. He gazed out over the 20 or so people looking back at him as his bandmates found their places. He tried to appear confident, like he'd done this all before, but the truth was, until that August night in 1991, he'd never set foot on a stage in front of a live audience. For the last few days they'd been rehearsing in the basement, but now they'd reached the top – of the Boardwalk at least. The trouble was, even this small crowd hadn't come to see a local foursome calling themselves Oasis; they were just the support act for a band from Birmingham called Sweet Jesus who were being tipped for stardom. Oasis had four songs with which to make an impression. Four songs for their new frontman, Liam, to prove he'd been worth gambling on.

Unbeknown to the 19-year-old warbler, his older brother, Noel, was watching from the balcony. He'd just returned home to the grey streets of Manchester after being fired from his job as a roadie for the Inspiral Carpets during their world tour. Before he got back to his mother's terraced house on Cranwell Drive, she'd told him something he was still struggling to believe: his cocky younger brother had joined a band. Liam, who never sang along to the radio, let alone showed any interest in music, was now fronting a group that had been going by the name of Rain until that night. There was no way Noel was going to miss the chance to see them perform, but as the evening drew on he toyed with the idea of leaving. Then Liam started to sing, and the course of British music was changed forever.

Madchester

Fittingly, for a working-class band that would go on to kick down the doors of the music establishment of the '90s, the seeds of Oasis were sown during a protest gig.

It was 1988, and Manchester was in the grip of the 'Madchester' cultural scene that blended indie rave and rock with acid house and the strains of the 1960s. But it wasn't just the alternative music of bands like The Happy Mondays and The Smiths that shook the city's cobbled streets. A spirit of defiance was coursing through Manchester. In response to a controversial move by the Tory government to suffocate the promotion of homosexuality, over 20,000 people had taken to the streets in February of that year to protest against Clause 28, and a few months later The Stone Roses played a benefit gig at the International 2 arena in an effort to raise funds to continue the fight. Among the fans roaring their approval of lead singer Ian Brown as his Mancunian lilt drifted from the stage were Liam and Noel Gallagher.

Mesmerised by the swagger of this strutting frontman, Liam, who was 15 and had recently been expelled from school, experienced a sensation that would transform his life. For it was as he watched Brown belting out another song that he realised that he wanted to experience the same thrill of a crowd screaming his name. No more lounging about at home watching daytime TV and dreaming of better things; he was going to do whatever it took to become a rock 'n' roll star.

Meanwhile, Noel, who was attending the gig separately from his brother, struck up a conversation with Graham Lambert, a guitarist in another of the

OPPOSITE: A young Noel leans against a poster advertising an upcoming Oasis gig in Amsterdam, February 1994. In the end, he was the only member of the band who made it to the Dutch capital – the rest were deported back to the UK after being arrested for fighting with football fans on the ferry over

BELOW: The Gallagher family: Noel (left), Paul, Liam (right) and their mother, Peggy, photographed in the 1970s

so-called Madchester bands, the Inspiral Carpets, who was attempting to record the performance. Their chance meeting eventually led to Noel unsuccessfully auditioning to join the Carpets, instead becoming a roadie for the band and receiving an education in the world of music that would pay off handsomely later.

After hanging out with local band Rain for a year or so, Liam finally got his chance to lead from the front in 1991 when they held auditions for a new singer. Impressed by Liam's vocals, Paul "Bonehead" Arthurs, Tony McCarroll, and Paul "Guigsy" McGuigan recruited him, and they were soon slated to perform at the Boardwalk – their first gig with Liam.

Sibling rivalry

In light of their stratospheric success in the mid-90s, one would be forgiven for assuming that Liam and his bandmates stunned the small gathering hovering around the bar that night at the Boardwalk with their memorable lyrics and his unique, nasally voice – but they didn't. Far from it. Later describing the performance as his "hardest gig ever", Liam lamented the pressures of "trying to act like Mick Jagger in front of your mates". However, the band did make an impression on one person: Noel, who was invited to join them, a proposition to which he promptly agreed on the condition that he could write the songs.

Recalling Liam's performance that night, Noel was characteristically honest: "As the songs got better, he got better. When I started writing the songs, I was writing songs and quickly sussed out the entire key structure was too low for Liam. So when you hear the early stuff, the songs are not very good, and he's not very good, but as I'm starting to write better songs for him, we all got better at the same time."

With Noel on board, the band finally had the guiding hand it needed. But he wasn't technically joining Rain: he was becoming part of Oasis – and Liam was determined to remind his brother that it was his band.

Hanging on the brothers' bedroom wall was an Inspiral Carpets poster that listed venues the band had played in 1991. Among them was the Swindon Oasis Leisure Centre. In a move that forever altered music history, Liam suggested to his bandmates that they change their name to Oasis – although he later insisted that he was never a member of Rain in the first place. "Obviously, they were called the Rain, but we had to stop that name. I was never in Rain, we were in Oasis. The day I joined it was Oasis!"

Regardless of the precise timings of the name change, what is beyond doubt is that none of this would ever have happened had two squabbling brothers not gone to see the Stone Roses back in '88.

"Without the Roses, there would have not been Oasis," said Noel in a later interview, "because I don't think Liam would have bothered joining Bonehead's group, and subsequently, I wouldn't have bothered joining Liam's group."

As the summer of 1991 turned to autumn, Oasis embarked on their first studio recording session, a five-piece band with dreams of one day making it big. But if they were going to break into the charts and beam their edgy, unapologetically rough, and instantly memorable songs around the world, they were going to have to fight their way to the front. Literally…

RIGHT: The band pose for a backstreet photo, November 1993. Within a year they'd be household names. After being taken under the wing of Jonny Marr of The Smiths, Oasis were introduced to his manager, Marcus Russell, after Marr convinced him to come and see them perform at the Hop and Grape in Manchester. When Noel later heard that Russell had been in the crowd, he called Russell and asked to meet him in London: "You get my train fare and I'll be with you in two hours." The two hit it off, and Russell became the band's manager, a role he would fulfil for 16 successful years

ABOVE: Going Dutch: Oasis on tour in the Netherlands in 1994

The doorman stationed outside King Tut's Wah Wah Hut was having none of it. Tasked with standing guard at the entrance to the Glasgow club on a drizzly Monday evening, he wasn't about to let a load of argumentative Mancunians barge their way in – even if a few of them looked ready for a brawl.

Oasis had piled into a couple of vans that morning and headed up to Scotland with another Manchester band, the Sister Lovers, who had a slot booked at the venue. Accounts vary, with some people claiming the owners of the Hut knew to expect an extra band, while others say Oasis turned up unannounced and asked to be allowed in. According to Tony McCarroll, one of the friends accompanying the band – a figure who was known affectionately as Big 'Un – threatened to fight his way inside if needed. Whatever the truth may be, the situation was finally resolved by a local music mogul who overheard the disagreement outside and told Oasis they could play four songs before the other acts came on. That man was Alan McGee, and his life, and those of Oasis, was about to change forever.

A co-founder of Creation Records, McGee was at the Hut to watch another band signed to his label, 18 Wheeler, but within moments of Oasis stepping off the stage after singing 'Rock 'n' Roll Star', 'Bring It on Down', 'Up in the Sky' and a cover of 'I Am the Walrus', he was scrabbling to secure another.

"The last song they did was the cover of 'I Am The Walrus' and right then I knew I wanted them on Creation," McGee recalled of that fateful night. "They wandered out afterwards, and I went up to Noel. I said: 'Have you got a record contract?' I just knew I had to have them on Creation. They were awesome, even then."

In an act of characteristic bravado, Oasis agreed to sign on for six albums with Creation despite knowing they only had enough songs for one. Work began on their first just a few months later at the Pink Museum in Liverpool, where Noel penned 'Supersonic', the band's debut single, over dinner. It would be released in April 1994 to wide acclaim and set many a tongue wagging about this strutting new band, but the moment that arguably propelled them to nationwide recognition came that June.

No maybe about it

By the summer of 1994, Oasis were a battle-hardened touring band committed to relentless performances across the UK. They'd even done their first international gig at Erotika in Paris. Yet while they were playing in front of ever-larger crowds, the prospect of entertaining thousands of people at the biggest music festival of the year would be enough to daunt any band – except Oasis.

As the crowd jostled in front of the NME Stage at Glastonbury that Sunday morning, Liam casually waltzed out with a can of beer clutched in one

hand and a tambourine in the other. Gazing out from behind a pair of shades at the festivalgoers, he growled, "Are you gonna wake up then, yeah? Some real songs," before launching into 'Bring It on Down'. They sounded gritty, punky, provocative, a band that knew they were on the cusp of greatness and had no compunction about telling the world.

After finishing their set with 'I Am the Walrus', they departed the stage with a nonchalant "see ya later" to the sound of rapturous applause, their place in the annals of Glastonbury and Britpop history cemented.

Just three days later, millions of eyes were trained on them again when they appeared on *Top of the Pops*. Everything was building up towards the moment that would send Oasis into the stratosphere and place them on equal footing with Britpop royalty and longtime rivals, Blur.

On 29 August 1994, Oasis's debut album, *Definitely Maybe*, hit the shelves of music stores across Britain. Within days it had sold over 100,000 copies en route to becoming the fastest-selling UK debut album at the time. A stunning riposte to the grungy sounds emanating from across the pond, it beautifully combined Liam's signature snarl with luscious, heavy guitar in an explosion of swagger and optimism that jolted the British music scene into a different dimension.

Blur, the undisputed kings of Britpop, now faced a worthwhile adversary. Both bands were recognised at the BRIT Awards in early 1995, with Blur bagging four awards (the most of any artist on one night at the time) while Oasis secured the gong for Best British Newcomer. The bands would continue to clash throughout the year, one that also saw drummer McCarroll depart Oasis a few months before they headlined Glastonbury.

Varying reasons for McCarroll's sudden exit have been put forth, with some accounts claiming that Noel didn't think McCarroll had the ability to drum on the more complex songs he was writing. Unsurprisingly, McCarroll told a different story, stating that it was personality clashes that ultimately saw him "unlawfully expelled" from the band (the feud would lead to a legal wrangle and an out-of-court settlement in 1999).

With Alan White now on board, Oasis continued their campaign to summit the charts. The simmering tensions between Blur and Oasis saw fans divided into two camps as the battle for Britpop supremacy was splashed across newspapers and airwaves, and in August of that year Blur made a move that would escalate the situation to fever pitch when they announced that they would be releasing their single 'Country House' on the same day that Oasis's 'Roll with It' came out.

This deliberate provocation drew a clear line in the sand, and when 'Country House' snatched the number-one spot, Oasis were devastated. But while Blur had undoubtedly won the battle, they were about to lose the war.

LEFT: A group portrait taken in November 1993

CLOCKWISE FROM OPPOSITE (TOP LEFT): Oasis play in the Splash Club at the Water Rats pub in London, 27 January 1994. Performing in front of a packed room that contained several journalists, the gig is considered the band's breakthrough moment in the capital; Tony McCarroll snapped backstage at a venue, 1994. By April 1995, he'd be replaced as the band's drummer; A young Liam displays his allegiance to Manchester City FC by sporting a vintage club shirt under his jacket; Liam jokingly sticks his tongue out at a picture of Stone Roses' frontman Ian Brown featured in a copy of the *New Musical Express* (*NME*)

LEFT: Looking every inch the rock star, Liam grips the mic during a show in Portsmouth, England, 2 May 1994

CLOCKWISE FROM OPPOSITE:
Outside 12 Flitcroft Street, Soho, London, 17 March 1994; Liam sips a beer inside the Oasis Bar in the King's Head Hotel, Newport, Wales, 3 May 1994. Oasis were touring to promote 'Shakermaker', their second single and a song that references Sifters Records, the shop the Gallagher brothers spent hours in browsing records as teenagers; Cityzens: Noel and Liam don Manchester City's home and third kit respectively. Huge fans of the club, both are regularly seen at City games

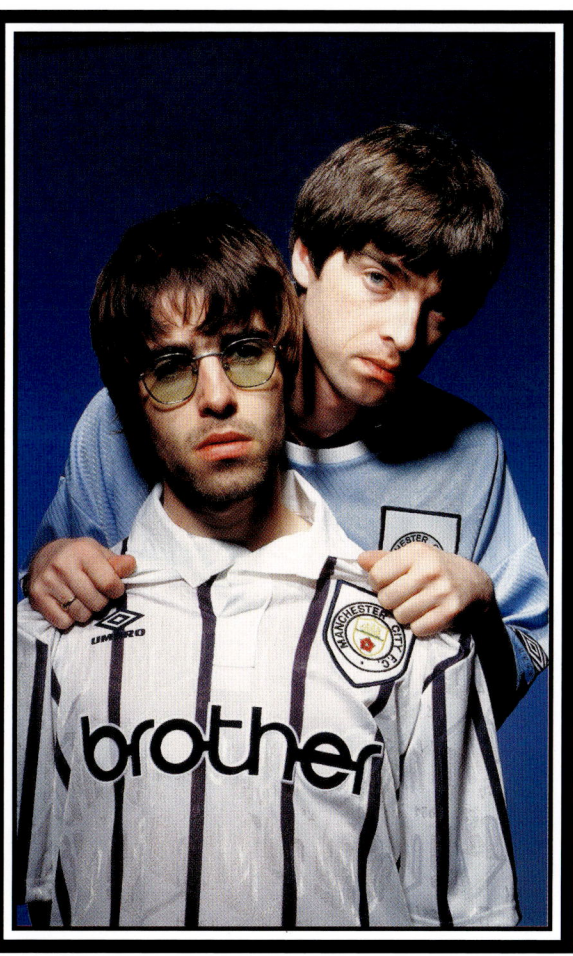

OASIS: THE STORY

ABOVE: Cap it off: Liam messes around in a shower cap while on tour in Wales, 1994

LEFT: "What you looking at?" Backstage at a music venue in London, 1994

RIGHT: Bring it on down: Oasis pose on an escalator at the Arndale shopping centre in Manchester. Taken by Kevin Cummings, this photo featured in an issue of *Vox* magazine

ABOVE: The importance of being idle: Oasis relax outside a cafe on Frith Street in London, 17 March 1994

Image: Getty

ABOVE: The iconic cover for Oasis's debut album, *Definitely Maybe*, was shot by photographer Michael Spencer Jones in Bonehead's flat. It was Jones who suggested that Liam lay on the floor having been inspired by the Egyptology section of the Manchester Museum. The 'wine' in the glass is actually diluted Ribena

RIGHT: Oasis play a gig inside a music store to promote their first album. Evan Dando of American band The Lemonheads can be seen on the right behind Noel

ABOVE: Noel scribbles a message onto a guitar during a record signing in a Virgin Megastore in Paris, 1995

LEFT (TOP): Putting their rivalry aside, Noel and Damon Albarn of Blur celebrate their *NME* Brat Award wins. Founded in 1953 as the *NME* Awards, they were briefly renamed Brat to poke fun at the BRIT Awards. Oasis would scoop four in 1996

LEFT (BOTTOM): Noel and girlfriend, Meg Mathews, together in February 1995. They would marry in Las Vegas two years later and welcome their daughter, Anaïs, in 2000

BELOW: A thoughtful-looking Liam takes a seat while Oasis play The Academy in New York City, 8 March 1995

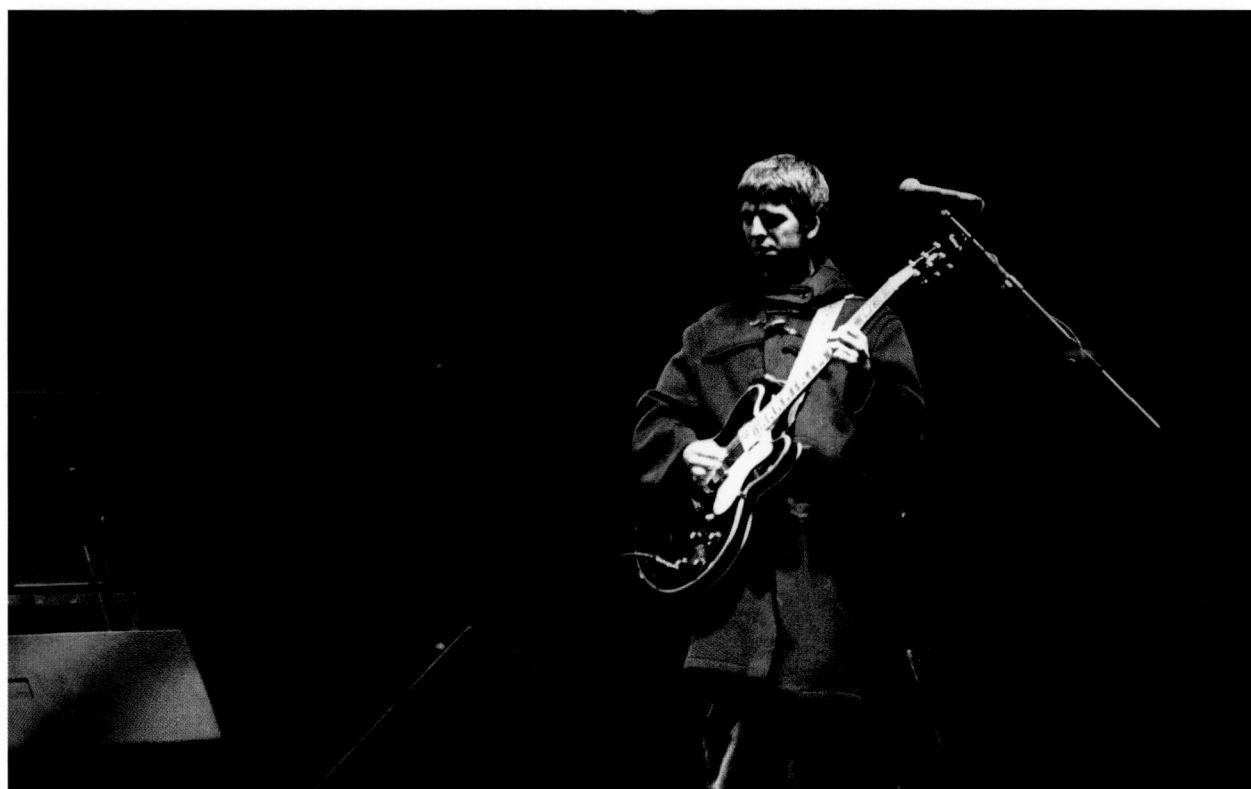

OPPOSITE: With a tambourine hanging from his neck, Liam sings beneath the lights at Glastonbury 1995, which Oasis headlined

LEFT: Noel strums away on the Main Stage at Glastonbury. Oasis's performance would later be hailed as one of their greatest

BELOW: Liam leans on Bonehead during their Glastonbury slot. Oasis played several songs from their upcoming album, *(What's the Story) Morning Glory?*, which was released in October of that year

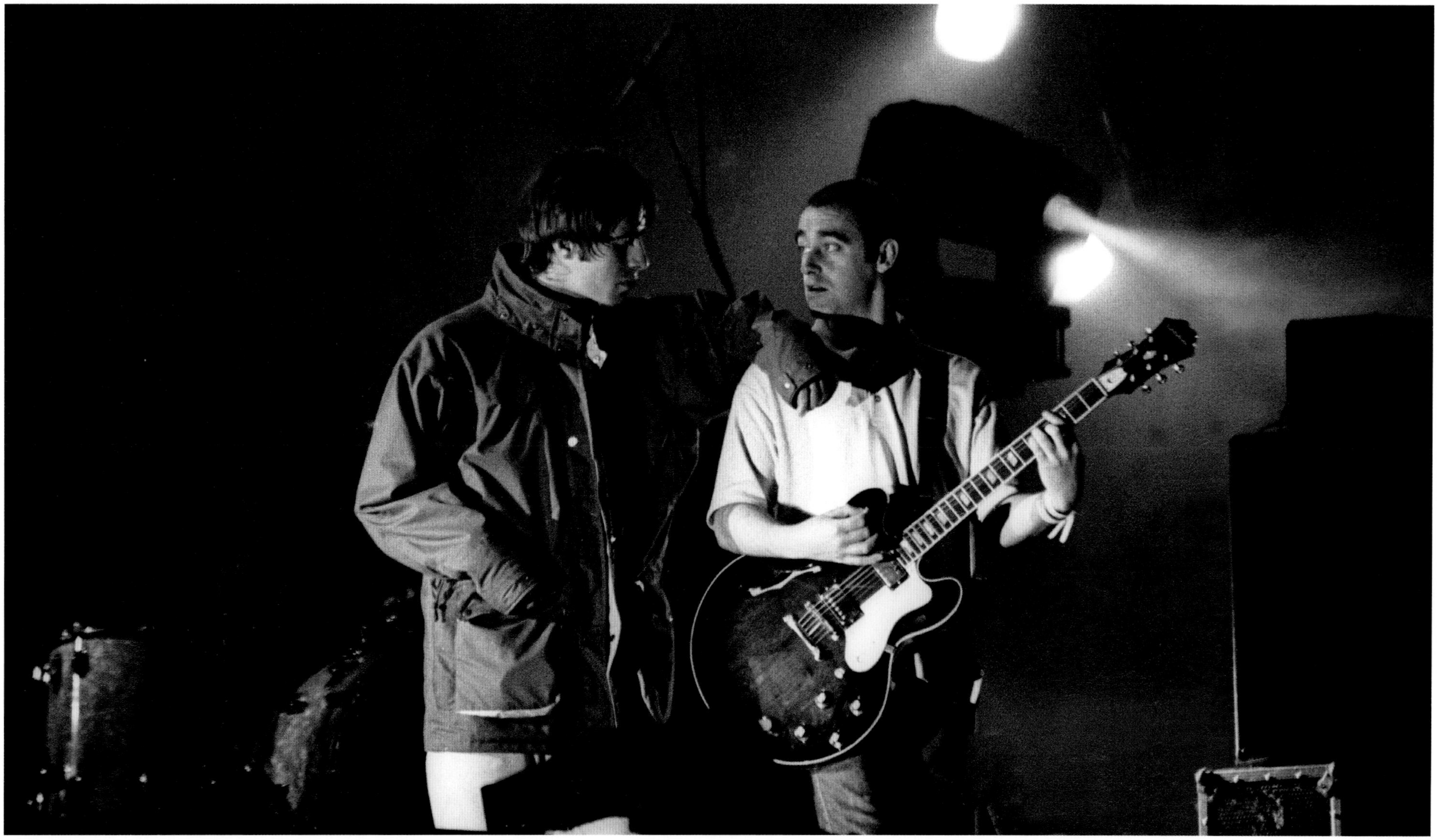

Images: Alamy

BELOW: Backstreet brooding: Paul "Bonehead" Arthurs, 2 August 1994. He was given his nickname as a child due to his parents' insistence on him having his hair cut very short

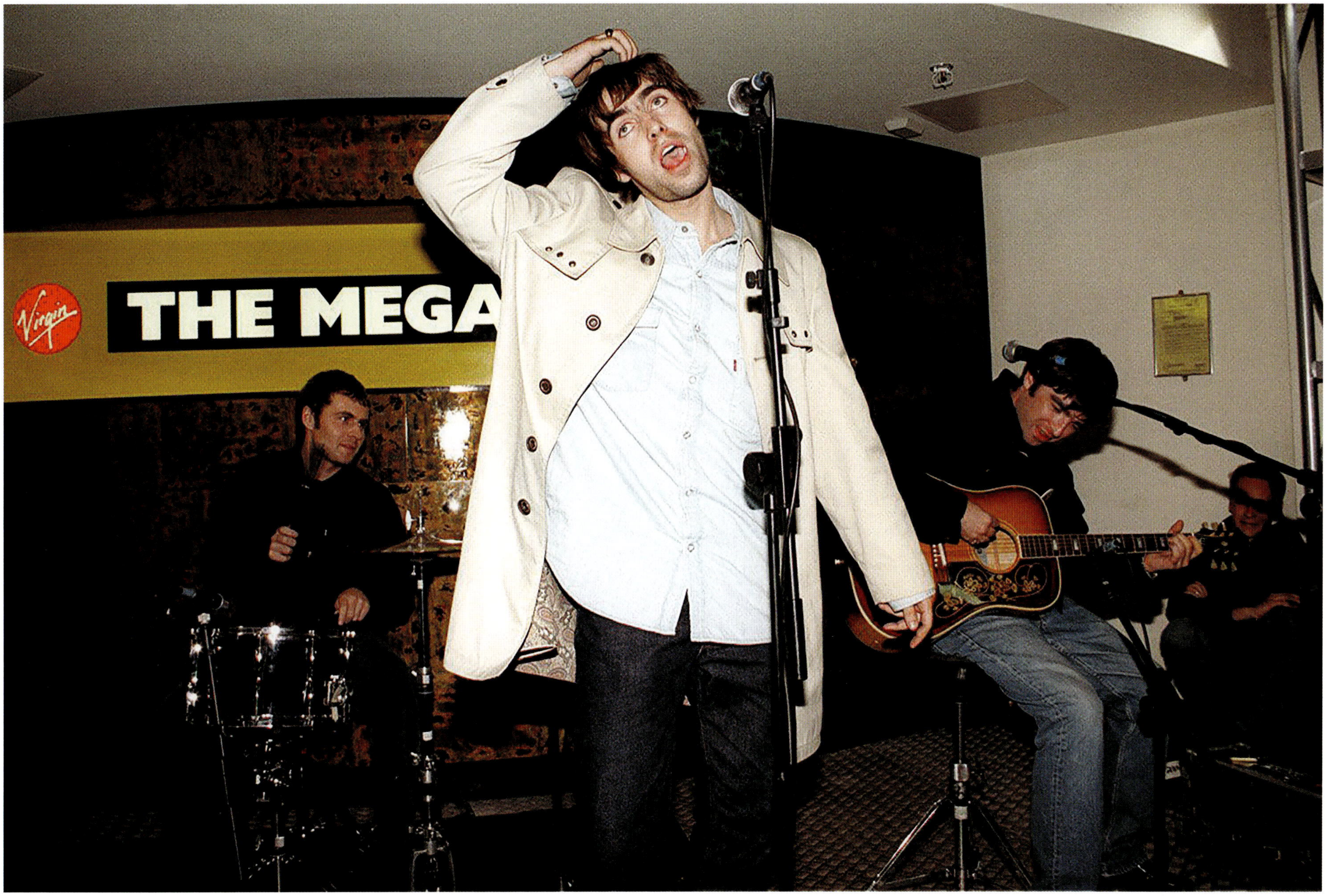

CLOCKWISE FROM ABOVE:
Oasis launch *(What's The Story) Morning Glory?* at the Oxford Street Virgin Megastore, 2 October 1995; Oasis emerge from a giant telephone box at the start of their 1995 performance at Earl's Court; The cover of *(What's The Story)* features DJ Sean Rowley crossing paths with Brian Cannon (right) – who designed the album sleeve – on Berwick Street in London. In the background, Owen Morris, who produced the album, can be seen holding its master tape in front of his face

Images: Getty, Alamy

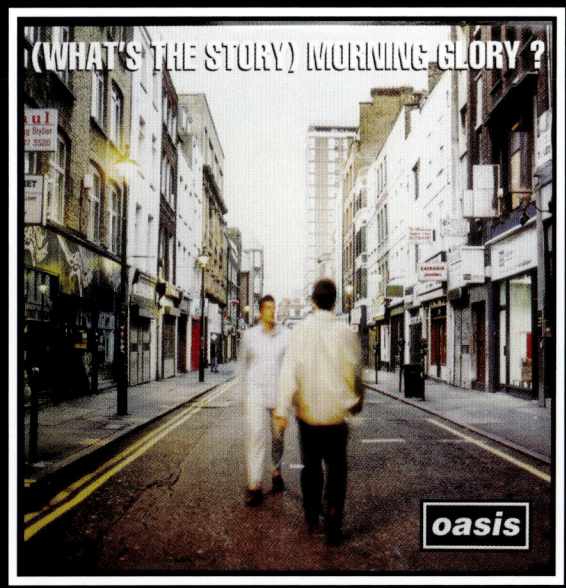

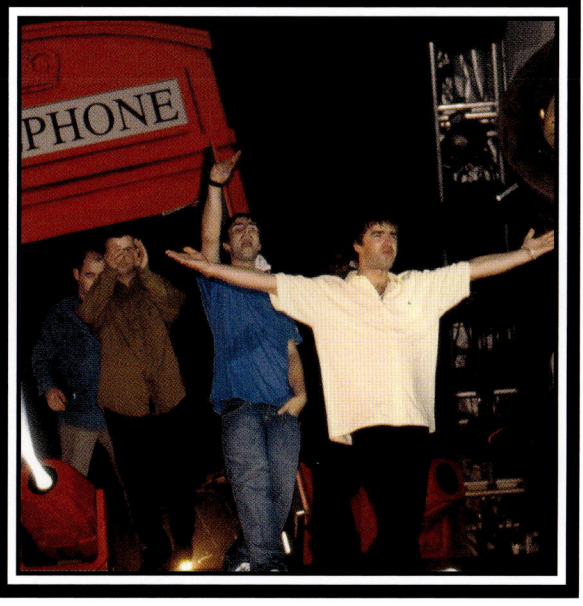

Oasis were already one of the biggest bands in the world by 1996. Fresh off the back of the incredible success of their second album, *(What's the Story) Morning Glory?*, which had sold a whopping 347,000 copies in the first week of its release in October 1995, Oasis had played to a record (in Europe) indoor crowd over two nights at Earl's Court. Yet despite achieving global fame and fortune, there was still the question of defeating Blur once and for all, and the opportunity to make their dominance of the charts official arrived on 19 February at the BRIT Awards.

On a night that would forever be remembered for a mocking rendition of 'Park Life' by the triumphant Gallaghers, Oasis scooped three awards: British Album of the Year, British Video of the Year (for 'Wonderwall'), and British Group. Better yet, they beat Blur in all three categories.

In less than three years, Oasis had gone from bargaining their way into a club in Glasgow to releasing two record-setting albums, headlining Glastonbury, and now winning the biggest prizes the British music industry had to offer. Surely it couldn't get any better than this.

Knebworth

Even if the thud of the helicopter's propellers hadn't drowned everything out, Oasis wouldn't have been able to make themselves heard. They were speechless as they gazed down at the army of fans occupying the field beside Knebworth House. Some were calling it the Woodstock of the '90s. Others labelled it the rock concert of the decade. Over two balmy August nights in Hertfordshire, Oasis were going to perform to 250,000 people at an event that sold out in a matter of minutes after roughly five per cent of the UK population rushed to buy tickets.

Clad all in white and with his arms outstretched like a long-promised messiah, Liam strode purposefully out onto the stage and soaked up the roar of the crowd – a crowd unlike any other ever seen before in the UK. If the albums and awards hadn't already done so, this crowning achievement solidified Oasis as *the* Britpop band, a genre that had now reached its zenith. It seemed like the world had come to worship at the altar of the Gallaghers, and while they would continue to taste success for years to come, nothing ever came close to those glorious summer nights when everything felt possible, a fleeting, shimmering moment when Oasis were the voice of a hopeful generation.

RIGHT: Liam belts out another classic at Balloch Castle Country Park, Loch Lomond, Scotland

OPPOSITE: White sets the pace on stage in Cardiff during his first-ever tour with Oasis, 18 March 1996

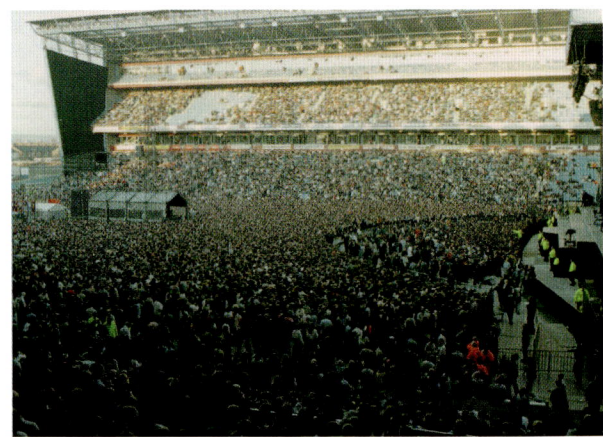

ANTICLOCKWISE FROM ABOVE: Over two sold-out nights on 27 and 28 April, around 80,000 people packed out Maine Road to watch local boys Oasis; Rule Britannia! A beaming Noel plays at Maine Road, the former home of his beloved Manchester City; Top of the table: a relaxed-looking Noel snapped in London, 1995

CLOCKWISE FROM BELOW: Have some of that: Liam throws beer at a photographer during a charity football competition at Mile End Stadium, London. The Oasis team would go down 2-1 to Blur's side; Liam takes it all in during a performance at Terminal 1 in Munich, 27 March 1996; Liam mocks the crowd at the 1996 BRIT Awards

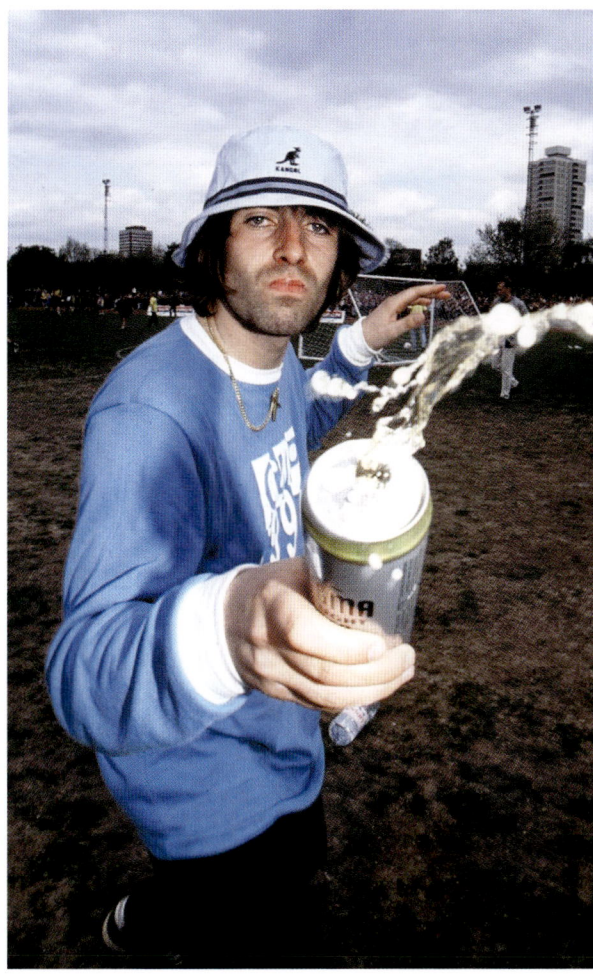

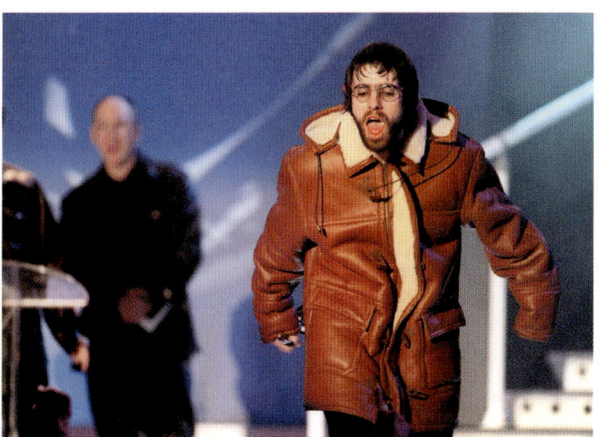

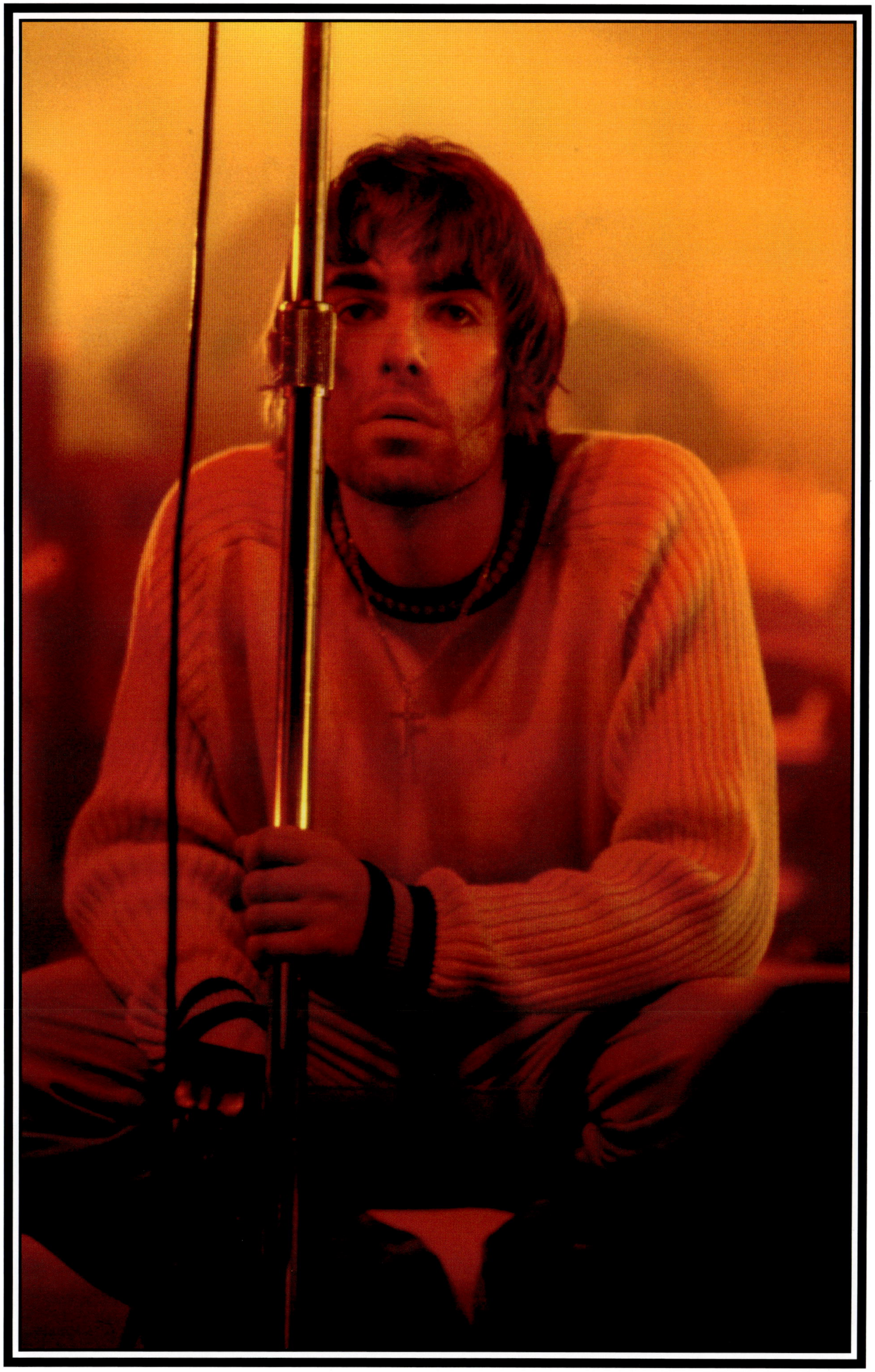

Images: Getty, Alamy

CLOCKWISE FROM OPPOSITE: Touring the grounds of Knebworth Park; A golden ticket: millions tried to buy one for Knebworth; A bright-eyed Paul "Bonehead" Arthurs gazes out at the crowd; Liam adopts his trademark pose; Around 125,000 fans attended each night at Knebworth. "I don't think we'd done 10,000 hours [practice] by the time we walked out at Knebworth, so we had no fear," Noel later recalled. "If we were doing Knebworth tomorrow, we'd be petrified"

Images: Getty, Alamy

TOP & OPPOSITE: Rocking on *The White Room*, a live show on Channel 4. Hosted by Radio 1 DJ Mark Radcliffe, the show aired from 1995-96 and featured both upcoming and established artists. Oasis, who featured on the show twice, were accompanied by the string section of an orchestra for Noel's performances of 'Don't Look Back in Anger' and 'Wonderwall'

ABOVE: The man who made it all happen: Alan McGee didn't waste a moment when it came to securing Oasis for Creation Records. After leaving his role at British Rail in 1983, McGee co-founded the label, which took its name from a '60s band called The Creation. The label would release several critically acclaimed albums, but by the early 1990s it was in serious financial trouble, leading McGee to sell half of the label to Sony in 1992. The success of Oasis's early albums reversed Creation's fortunes, but the label closed in 1999

FAR LEFT: Liam enjoys a cigarette while attending a Sex Pistols gig at Finsbury Park in London, 23 June 1996

CENTRE: Liam riles up the audience at the 1996 MTV Video Music Awards Show at Radio City Music Hall in New York City. Following an expletive-laden rendition of 'Champagne Supernova', Liam got into a row with Noel, spat out some beer he'd been swigging, threw down his microphone, and stropped off with the song yet to be finished

ABOVE: Giving the press two fingers on a night out with then fiancée, Patsy Kensit

CLOCKWISE FROM TOP LEFT: Fans queue to buy tickets for Oasis's Be Here Now Tour, 26 July 1997. Many people slept overnight in the line to ensure they bagged one of the 156,000 UK tickets available, all of which sold out in a couple of hours; Released on 21 August 1997, *Be Here Now* was the best-selling album of that year in the UK, with almost 1.5 million sales. Its intriguing cover, which features a submerged Rolls Royce and a moped, cost £75,000 to create; Noel and Meg arrive with Alan McGee at a Downing Street drinks party hosted by newly elected prime minister, Tony Blair. Noel later confessed that his decision to attend was influenced by narcotics: "Being famous is a good laugh when you're on drugs. You meet people and go 'Nah, nah, fucking, nah' and everyone goes, 'Wow, hasn't he got loads of charisma?' And really, you're just hammered."; Noel and Liam's estranged father, Tommy, poses with a copy of *Be Here Now*. The brothers cut ties with their father, who physically abused them and their mother

CLOCKWISE FROM OPPOSITE (BOTTOM LEFT): The set for the Be Here Now Tour regularly featured a giant telephone box; Shake it, baby: Liam wields a tambourine on stage at the Aberdeen Exhibition and Conference Centre, Scotland, September 1997; On tour in Milan, Italy, November 1997; Noel crouches behind an unimpressed Liam on *The Tonight Show With Jay Leno*. Oasis played 'Don't Go Away' on the hit US show; Leathered: Noel and Liam at the Lyceum Theatre in London, September 1998

CLOCKWISE FROM OPPOSITE (TOP LEFT): Noel collects the Best Band of the Decade prize at the *Loaded* Awards, London, May 1999; Liam greets a bank of press photographers at a party in Cannes, France, 16 May 1999; The Gallaghers doing what they do best at Ancienne Belgique, a concert hall in Brussels, Belgium, 23 March 2000; Down but not out: Liam and Noel convene a press conference at the Water Rats pub in London in the wake of Paul McGuigan quitting the band via fax – just a fortnight after Bonehead had announced his own departure. "We've been left holding the shite sandwich," lamented Noel – but Oasis would live on

CLOCKWISE FROM OPPOSITE (FAR LEFT): "Chew what, mate?" Liam bites on a tambourine while Oasis entertain a sell-out crowd at the Universal Amphitheatre in California, 9 April 2000; Grasping a vibrant Fender Telecaster guitar, Noel casually flicks the V-sign at the Reebok Stadium in Bolton, England, during the Standing on the Shoulder of Giants Tour, 15 July 2000; Oasis's fourth album sold over 310,000 units in the first week of its release. The title was inspired by a quote from Sir Isaac Newton, which Noel spotted on the side of a £2 coin; Britpop banner: fans go wild for Oasis at Wembley Stadium, 21 July 2000; Manhattan's world-famous Radio City Music Hall. Oasis played the venue in May 2000 and then again in 2001 as part of the Tour of Brotherly Love along with The Black Crowes and Spacehog, with all of the bands having brothers in their lineups

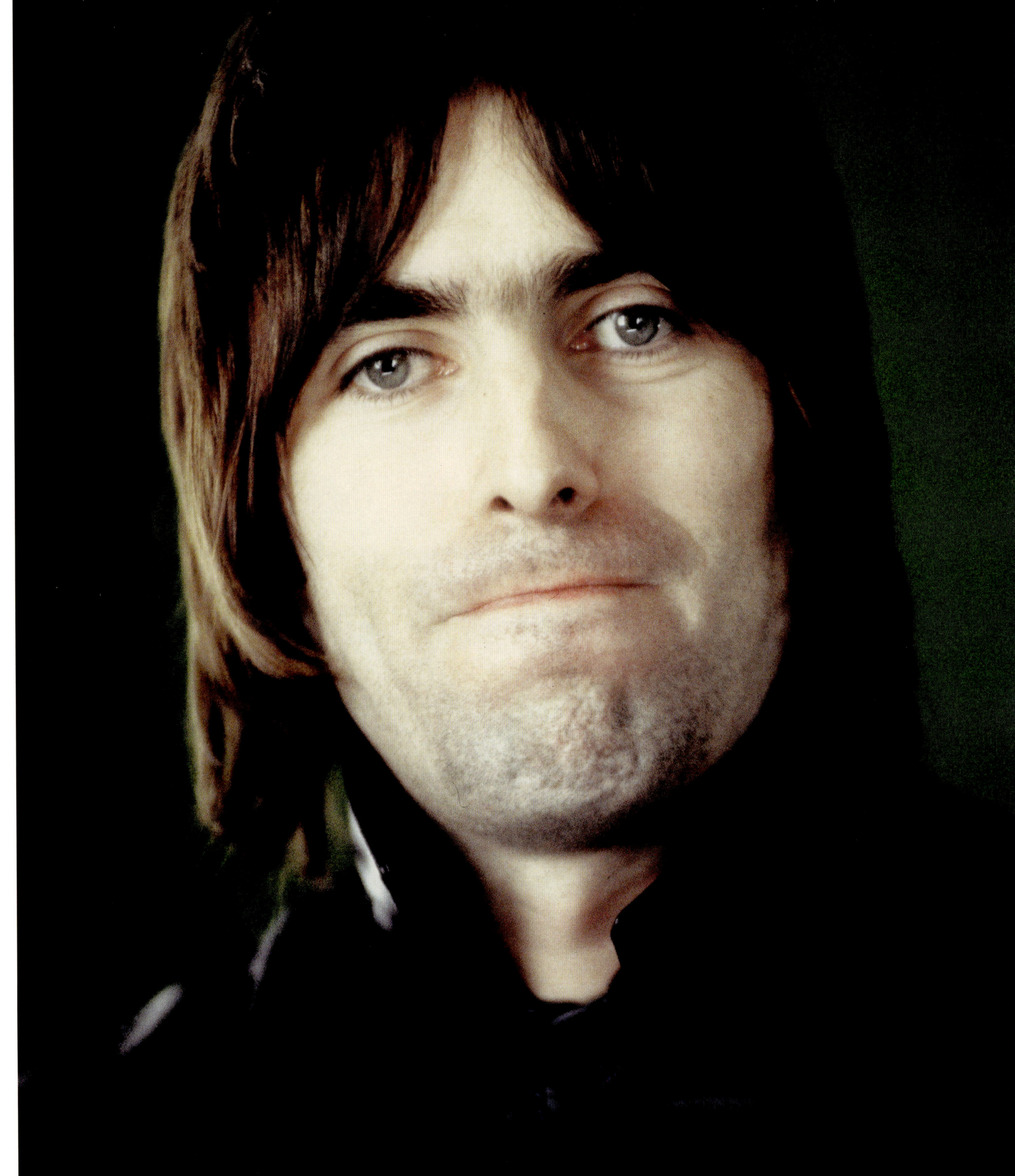

OPPOSITE: Liam almost manages a smile during a Paris photo shoot, 23 February 2000

ABOVE: Smoulder on: Noel leans in for the lens, 4 April 2002

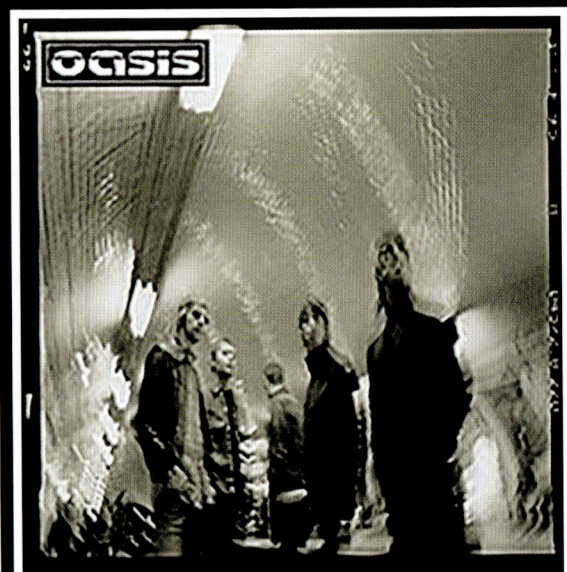

CLOCKWISE FROM ABOVE: The cover of *Heathen Chemistry*, Oasis's fifth studio album. Released on 1 July 2002, it was the final album on which Alan White played before leaving the band and the first to feature new additions Gem Archer (guitar) and Andy Bell (bass). Three months prior to the album's release, its 11 tracks were leaked online by an unknown individual. It would go on to be yet another commercial success; Noel on the set of the video for 'Little by Little'

BELOW: Beautiful day: Noel presents U2 with the Outstanding Contribution to Music Award at the BRIT Awards, 26 February 2001

Images: Getty, Alamy

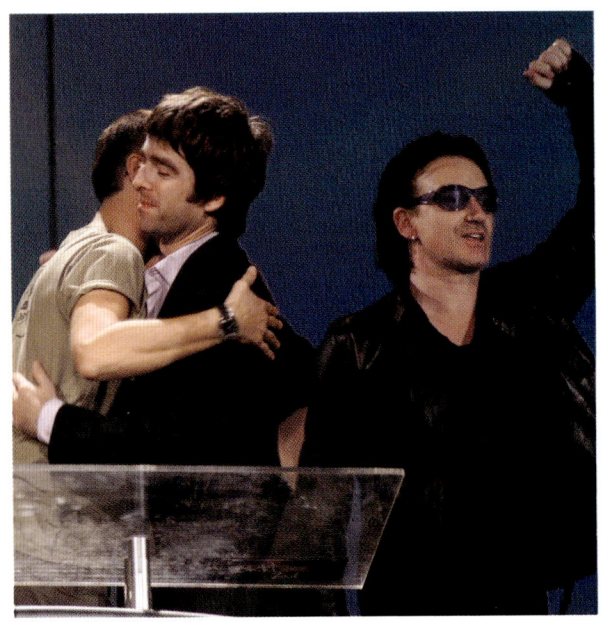

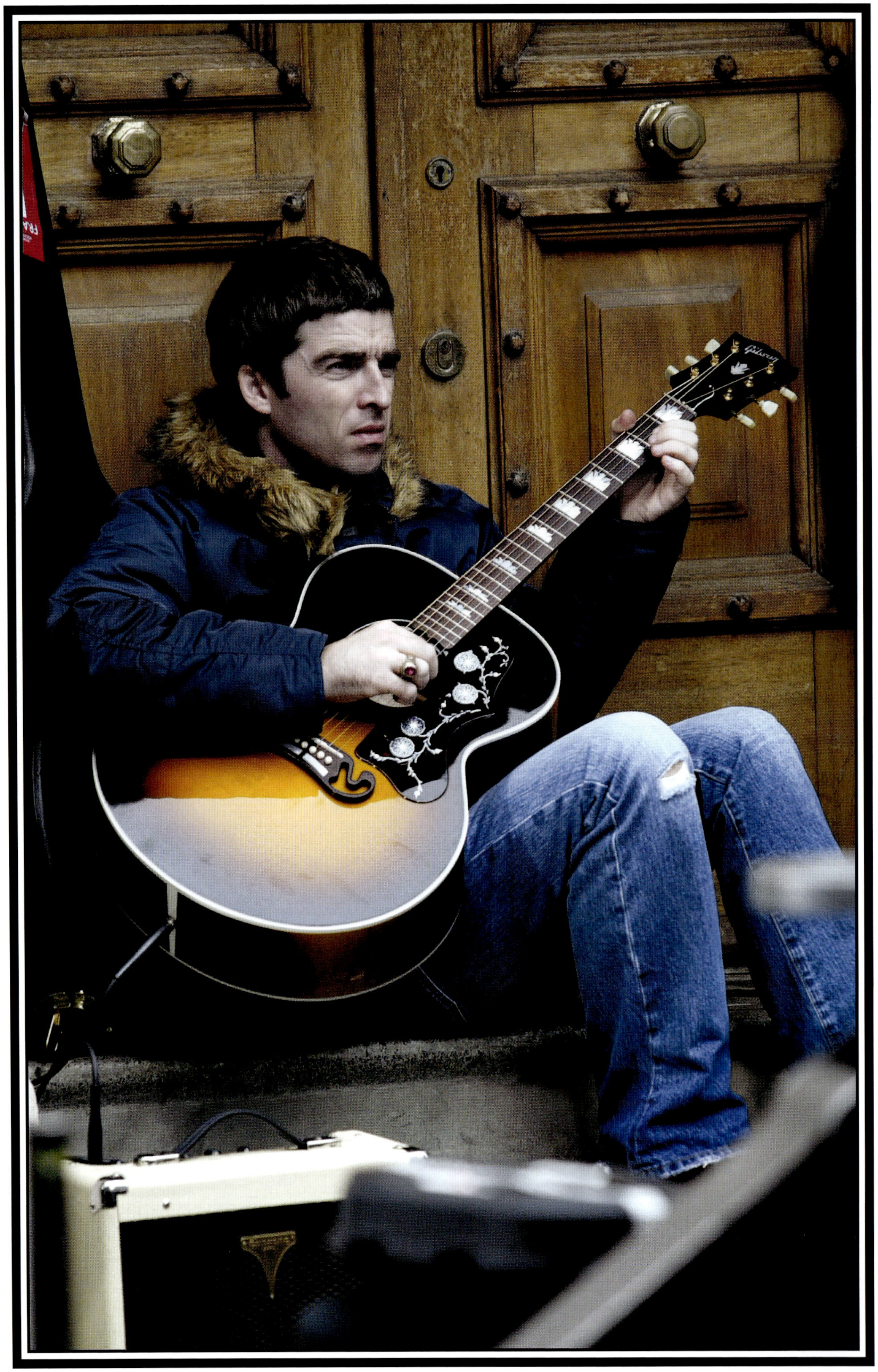

BELOW Liam sports in-ear monitors (used to help hear the music) at Glastonbury 2004 – a gig he wouldn't look back on fondly. "I've always enjoyed Glastonbury. There's only one that I didn't and that was when I wore a white jacket. I didn't enjoy that because that was when I'd first started using in-ears [monitors] and it's spun me out for 15 years. I hated that gig, man."

CLOCKWISE FROM BOTTOM LEFT:
Go let it out: Noel channels a higher power at the Shoreline Amphitheatre, California, 11 September 2005; Zak Starkey on drums at the Alcatraz in Milan, Italy, 12 May 2005; The first album to feature drummer Zak Starkey (filling in after Alan White's departure), *Don't Believe the Truth* was hailed as Oasis's best album in a decade when it hit shelves on 30 May 2005. It has since gone on to sell over 7 million copies, evening making a splash in America; Gem Archer plays guitar alongside Noel at the Shoreline; On stage at the London Astoria, 10 May 2005. Playing just a few weeks before *Don't Believe the Truth* was released, Oasis (who were supported by Yeti) opened with 'Turn Up the Sun' before going on to play other new songs including 'Lyla' and 'The Importance of Being Idle'

OASIS: THE STORY

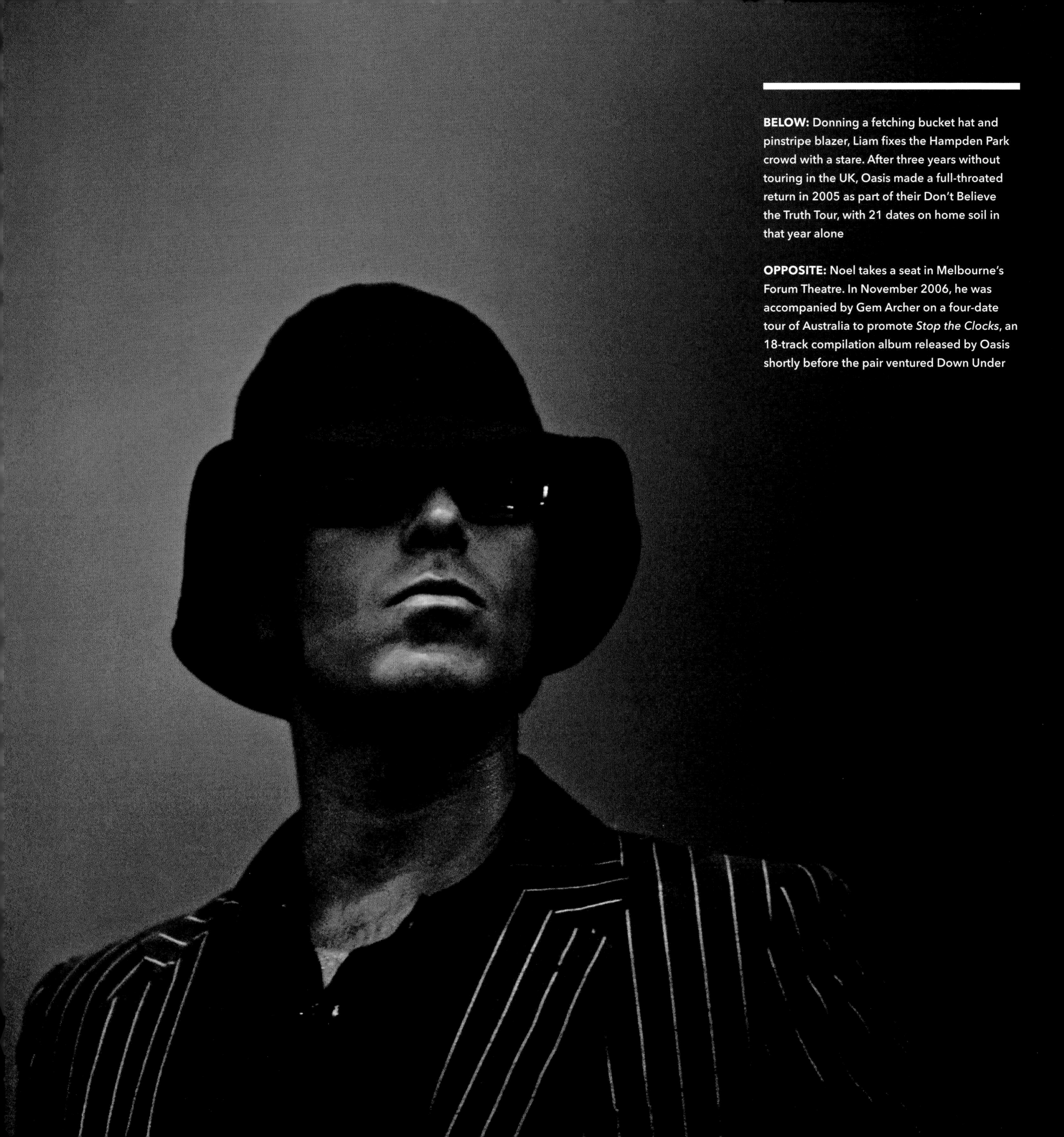

BELOW: Donning a fetching bucket hat and pinstripe blazer, Liam fixes the Hampden Park crowd with a stare. After three years without touring in the UK, Oasis made a full-throated return in 2005 as part of their Don't Believe the Truth Tour, with 21 dates on home soil in that year alone

OPPOSITE: Noel takes a seat in Melbourne's Forum Theatre. In November 2006, he was accompanied by Gem Archer on a four-date tour of Australia to promote *Stop the Clocks*, an 18-track compilation album released by Oasis shortly before the pair ventured Down Under

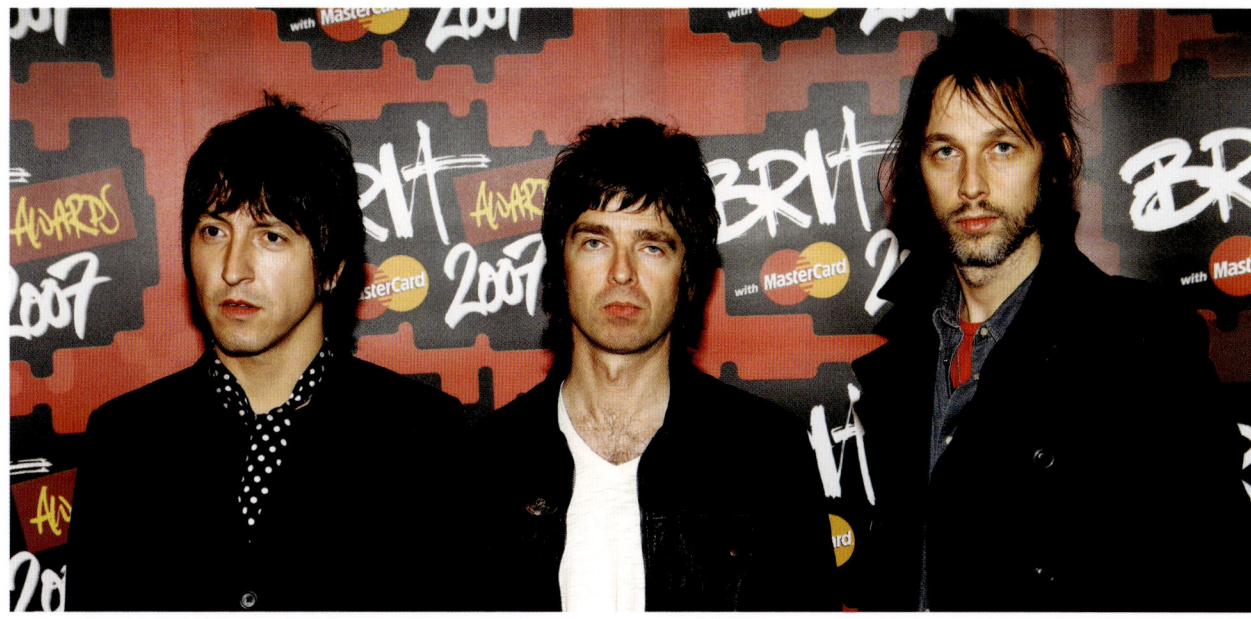

OPPOSITE: Live at the Odyssey Arena in Belfast. Despite tensions within the band, Oasis delivered another stellar show in August 2008

LEFT: Gem Archer (left), Noel, and Andy Bell arrive at the 2007 BRIT Awards, where Oasis would receive the award for Outstanding Contribution to Music

BELOW Belting! The Gallaghers celebrate with boxer and fellow Mancunian Ricky Hatton in the wake of his 2008 defeat of Paulie Malignaggi in a light welterweight clash at the MGM Grand Las Vegas

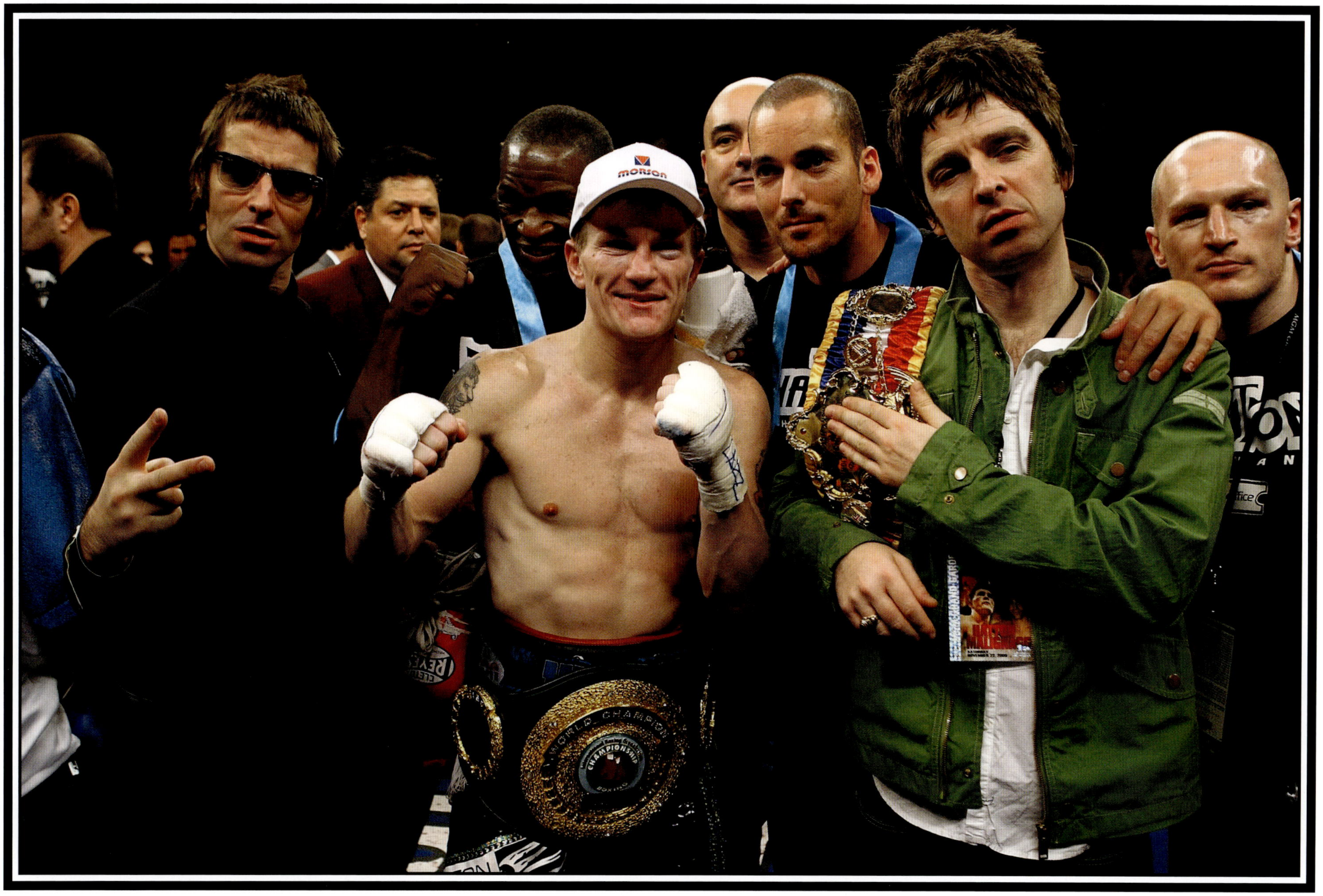

Images: Getty, Alamy

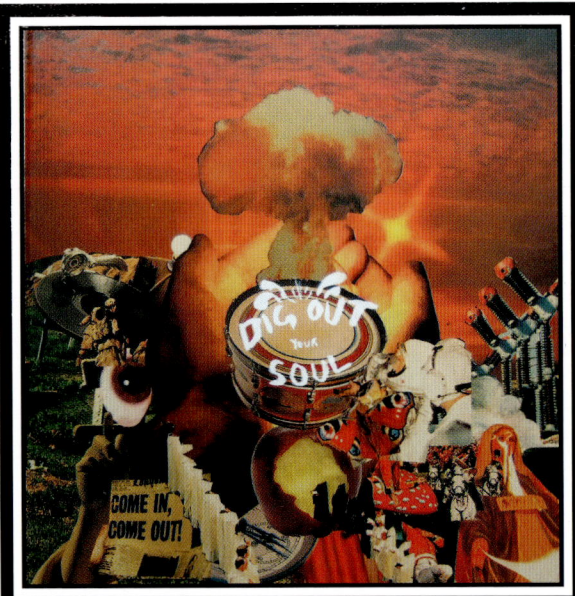

ABOVE: The final Oasis studio album, *Dig Out Your Soul,* marked a return to heavier rock. While Noel penned most of its tracks, Liam wrote 'I'm Outta Time', 'Ain't Got Nothin'' and 'Soldier On'. Debuting at number one in the UK album charts, it peaked at number five on the U.S. *Billboard* 200

RIGHT: On sacred ground: Oasis walk the Wembley pitch following an announcement that they would play three shows at the home of English football in 2009. They had previously appeared at Wembley in 2000, a time that Noel later remembered as "the low point in Oasis"

Image: Alamy

They'd swirled for years. New music. Secret meetings. An impending announcement that the Gallaghers had put their considerable differences aside and agreed to reunite. All of them rumours – rumours that bobbed to the surface only to disintegrate in the cold light of day. So why, in August 2024, would the music industry's affirmations of an Oasis reunion prove to be anything other than a false dawn? Except this time, things really were different.

A day after Liam had taken to X to tantalise fans with a post that read, "I never did like that word FORMER," the news broke: Oasis were back.

"The guns have fallen silent. The stars have aligned. The great wait is over. Come see. It will not be televised." So read the press release that confirmed Oasis Live '25, a tour that will – now additional dates have been added – see the band performing over 40 shows across the globe, including seven nights at London's Wembley Stadium.

As if proof of their enduring popularity was needed, approximately 14 million people tried to buy a ticket for one of the gigs on the UK and Ireland legs of the tour in the ensuing scramble that followed the announcement. Within ten hours all of them had been sold.

Never one to disappoint the online community, Liam joked about the day he reconnected with his brother: "It was a lovely day [sic] we shared our packed lunches together, we talked, giggled, cuddled and held hands, and scowled for the camera."

In reality, it wasn't a "great revelatory moment" that brought the Gallaghers back together but "the gradual realisation that the time is right". The timing couldn't have been better, coming 15 years to the day since Oasis had split and almost 30 years after the release of *Definitely Maybe*.

Keen to avoid media intrusion picking at old wounds, neither Liam nor Noel will be speaking to the press in the lead-up to the first reunion concert at Cardiff's Principality Stadium on 4 July. However, when questioned by a fan about whether a setlist circulating online that included 'Shakermaker', 'Stand by Me', and 'The Importance of Being Idle' was, in fact, the one the band would play on tour, Liam replied, "It's not far off."

Regardless of what they play, the return of Oasis marks a nostalgic celebration of a time when Britain hummed with the sound of fresh, exciting music and the anticipation of what lay ahead as a new millennium loomed on the horizon. Whatever else this year has in store, for the fans of Britpop's greatest band, the summer of 2025 is going to be supersonic.

OPPOSITE: The Gallaghers glare out from an electronic billboard announcing their upcoming shows at Wembley Stadium. Initially, they were due to play four nights at England's national stadium, but sheer demand for tickets will now see them performing a total of seven gigs at the venue, which has a capacity of 90,000

BELOW: Lazio fans display a banner welcoming the news of the Oasis reunion during their team's 2-2 draw against AC Milan, testament to the band's international appeal

CLOCKWISE FROM OPPOSITE: Noel leads his High Flying Birds in Atlanta, Georgia, April 2012; Liam attends the premiere of *Supersonic*, a 2016 documentary that explores Oasis's early years and the incredible success they enjoyed in the '90s; Liam on stage with Beady Eye, who released two albums; Pictured here on display in 2019 during the *Masterplan 25* exhibition, this is the front of the Rolls Royce that can be seen submerged in a swimming pool on the cover of Oasis's third album, *Be Here Now*

Image: Getty

It was a plum that did it. They'd had plenty of rows before, even come to blows, but when Liam launched a piece of fruit against the wall of the Oasis dressing room during the build-up to a performance in France, something inside Noel snapped. Thankfully, it wasn't a bone given that Liam then proceeded to snatch up a guitar and "swing it like an axe" before smashing it to pieces. As the rest of the band watched the younger Gallagher erupt, his brother silently made a choice: it was over.

Controversy was never a stranger where Oasis were concerned. From public outbursts to arrests, fights, and festival no-shows, the tensions that bubbled just beneath the surface only served to bolster the band's image as the bad boys of British rock. Their live shows crackled with anticipation as a result. Would they play to the end or start slinging insults? Not knowing which way things might go was part of the thrill of being an Oasis fan. But behind the scenes, the fallouts were beginning to take their toll, and the situation finally boiled over in August 2009.

While both Liam and Noel would later express their regrets over the argument that led to Noel quitting the band, at the time the older Gallagher was just glad to be out. "It's with some sadness and great relief to tell you that I quit Oasis tonight," he said in a statement released shortly after the explosive clash in Paris, which had resulted in the show they were due to play at the Rock en Seine festival being cancelled.

Candid as ever, Liam provided his own take on why his brother departed the band that had made them both fantastically wealthy and famous: "I didn't leave Oasis," he told Radio X. "Noel Gallagher left Oasis. He couldn't handle the vibes anymore. He couldn't handle the rock 'n' roll. He was too scared of it. So now he's gone all cosmic pop and Leo Sayer."

With contact between the two severed, Liam wasted little time in forming a new band with the other members of Oasis called Beady Eye. Noel followed suit by creating his own band a year later – Noel Gallagher's High Flying Birds. Yet while the two weren't speaking, both of them discussed the other in subsequent interviews, with Noel famously calling his brother "the angriest man you'll ever meet. He's like a man with a fork in a world of soup."

Despite the divide, rumours of a reunion persisted. After dismissing the idea in an interview with *Rolling Stone* magazine in 2013, Noel breathed new life into the prospect of the brothers once again working together when he told Radio X, "One should never say never, should one look like a bit of an idiot somewhere down the road, when you're waving a cheque for a quarter of a billion in *The Sun*!"

Nonetheless, the years rolled by without any sign of a rapprochement, even though Liam, who has become renowned for his amusing posts on X (formerly Twitter), asked his brother to "get the BIG O back together" in 2018. Noel's silence was deafening. Nine years on from their acrimonious split, hopes of a reunion were fading fast. They were all but dead and buried as the 15th anniversary of that chaotic night in Paris loomed. And then the rumours started again…

OPPOSITE: Pictured here shortly after Oasis's split in 2009, Liam strides through a lobby, cigarette in hand, bound for life without the band he'd fronted for 18 years. He immediately moved on with Beady Eye, but while they enjoyed success in the UK album charts, they disbanded in 2014. Former Oasis guitarist Gem Archer, who'd been part of Beady Eye, joined Noel Gallagher's High Flying Birds, who continue to perform together at the time of writing (February 2025)

Images: Getty